Three Million Mice

Three Million Mice

A Story of Modern Medical Research

by Ada and Frank Graham

illustrated with photographs
drawings by Robert Shetterly

Charles Scribner's Sons · New York

ACKNOWLEDGMENTS

This book could not have been written without the many courtesies and patient guidance extended to us by Dr. Edwin P. Les, Supervisor of Research and Development of the Jackson Laboratory.

Many other people at the Jackson Laboratory went out of their way to be helpful to us and explain their work in detail. We thank them all. In particular, we want to mention Dr. Terrie Cunliffe-Beamer, Susan Grindle, Priscilla Lane, Dr. Larry Mobraaten, and Karla Reed. For photographs, we are indebted to George McKay.

For readers who would like to learn about the laboratory in greater detail, we recommend *The First Fifty Years at the Jackson Laboratory* by Jean Holstein, a book that was published by the Jackson Laboratory, Bar Harbor, Maine, in 1979.

Library of Congress Cataloging in Publication Data
Graham, Ada.   Three million mice.
Includes index.
Summary: Describes the work of scientists at Jackson Laboratory, where mice are bred for laboratories and medical institutions all over the world and studied in connection with research in genetics and hereditary disease.
1. Mice as laboratory animals—Juvenile literature.
2. Mice—Breeding—Juvenile literature.   3. Jackson Laboratory (Bar Harbor, Me.)—Juvenile literature.   4. Medical research —United States—Juvenile literature.   [1. Mice as laboratory animals.   2. Jackson Laboratory (Bar Harbor, Me.)   3. Medical research.   4. Genetics]   I. Graham, Frank, date.   II. Shetterly, Robert, ill.   III. Title.
SF407.M5G7   619'.93   81-14338
ISBN 0-684-17150-3   AACR2

Printed in the United States of America

Contents

Preface: Laboratory Animals

Three million mice! Why mice? And why so many?

Familiar pets such as dogs and cats are often bought by laboratories and may be held for research under harsh conditions. Rare wild animals such as monkeys also are captured and subjected to painful experiments. Understandably, many people object to these practices.

But the mice described in this book have been bred as laboratory animals for dozens of generations, just as chickens and beef cattle are raised to supply us with food. These mice are treated humanely throughout their lives. By studying them, scientists are making important discoveries in the struggle to understand and cure human diseases.

Laboratory mice are bred chiefly to help us relieve human suffering. They take the place of cats, dogs, monkeys, and other animals that are far less suitable for this purpose. They are small and easily cared for. They breed quickly in captivity.

These are some of the reasons why mice have become the most important animals in modern medical research.

1 · The Mouse Room

The large, brightly lighted room was filled with rows of tall metal racks. Clear plastic cages stood on the racks' shelves, seven rows high. On each of the cages were colored tags and a filter hood that fitted closely over the top. Small animals moved busily about inside them.

A young woman, who wore a short, white laboratory dress, pushed a table on wheels between the rows of racks. She lifted one of the plastic cages from a shelf and set it on the table. When she removed the filter hood, she looked down into the two compartments of the cage. Each held a small water bottle and was covered by a metal screen. Attached to this cover was a feed container, or "hopper." Mice scampered through the wood shavings that lined the bottom of their cage.

The woman read the card on the cover of one compartment. It listed the number and the type of mice inside and gave her other information about them. Two pairs of long forceps stood in plastic jars of disinfectant on the table. She selected one of them and, working swiftly, caught one of the mice by its tail and lifted it from the box. (There is less chance of hurting an active

*An animal caretaker uses forceps
to remove a mouse from its cage.*

adult mouse if it is lifted by its sturdy tail than by any other part of its body.) Held gently but firmly by the forceps, the mouse squirmed and tried to set its feet on solid ground again.

The woman studied the mouse carefully for a moment. Its fur was gray brown, and it had large ears and beady little dark eyes, like all the other mice on the shelves nearby. The woman noted the animal's sex and assured herself that it was in good health. Then she lowered it lightly into a clean plastic box on the table. She picked up the other mouse in the compartment, studied it carefully, and then set it down beside its mate in the wood shavings that lined the new cage.

Until then, it had been an uneventful morning. The woman was an animal caretaker at the Jackson

Laboratory in Bar Harbor, Maine. She was doing the job that she did every day in one of the breeding rooms where mice are raised by the thousands. She had already handled more than a hundred cages, checking the mice and moving them to clean cages. She had furnished each of these cages with a fresh bottle of water and filled the hopper with feed from the large metal bin on her table.

Now she began to transfer the mice from the other compartment to a clean cage. Inside were a pair of adults and a litter of six baby mice, which she called "pups." She used the forceps to lift the parents by their tails and examine them in turn. Because the tails of the pups were still short and weak, she placed the forceps on their shoulders and moved them gently to their new home.

Suddenly, when lifting the last of the pups, she

The gray-brown color, large ears, and beady little eyes of this mouse indicate to lab workers that it is a normal, healthy specimen.

noticed that there was something different about it. It was smaller than the other young mice in the cage. When she put it down on the shavings, she saw that the little mouse kept moving to its left in a tight circle. The pup looked almost as if it were chasing its tail.

The woman filled out a card. On the card she wrote the cage number and a brief description of the animal's strange behavior: "Mouse small, moves in circles." Then she signed her name on the card and gave it to her supervisor.

By finding a special pup among the nearly 3 million mice that are raised at the Jackson Laboratory every year, this young woman may become a part of medical history. She lives in a small New England town, far from large cities, just as the other men and women do who work as animal caretakers with her. But her work is a part of some of the most advanced medical research taking place in our time. The mouse she picked out for special study may help to solve some of the mysteries that still puzzle doctors about human disease, birth defects, and heredity.

Today scientists are trying to help us understand who we are and what we are. Why are some of us tall and thin, and others short and plump? Why are some of us likely to get certain diseases, while others escape them? Why will some of us live longer than others?

Mice are born with different characteristics, too. Some mice are thin, some are fat. Some of these animals suffer from cancer or other disorders that are very much like human illnesses. Other mice live comparatively long and healthy lives.

Scientists have found that studying mice helps them understand some of the health problems of men and women. These animals are becoming the most important living research animals available to medical science. They are among the smallest of mammals. This makes them fairly easy to raise and care for in a limited amount of space. Yet, being mammals—warm-blooded, with backbones, and nursing their young—they are similar in many ways to human beings.

But their differences from us are important, too. They give birth to young often, sometimes as regularly as once a month. Their litters are usually large.

This last point is important because scientists need many animals to work with in their medical research. The laboratory supplies thousands of mice every week to its own scientists and to other medical institutions all over the world. But not just any mice. "Jax Mice," as Jackson Laboratory mice are called, are the royalty of laboratory animals. This is the story of Jax Mice and the people who have helped to make them famous.

2 · Jax Mice

"I used to drive past the Jackson Laboratory when I was a girl and I wondered just what went on in there," Susan Grindle said. "It had all of these large buildings here in Bar Harbor, right on the edge of Acadia National Park. I knew that it had something to do with medical research, and I had an idea that thousands of mice were running around all over the place. It was very mysterious."

Susan Grindle, a red-haired, enthusiastic young woman, is a room leader now at the laboratory. She is in charge of one of the large breeding rooms. Depending on the amount of work to be done, she has two and sometimes three animal caretakers working under her. She has been able to answer for herself most of the questions she used to ask about the laboratory.

"I was born in Bar Harbor, but I never realized that there were any really interesting jobs in the town," she said. "I knew it was a very beautiful place, with the sea on one side and the mountains on the other, but I left home to find work. I worked for some years in other parts of the country."

When there was a death in her family, Susan

An aerial view of the laboratory.

Grindle returned to Bar Harbor. She heard from friends that there were jobs to be had in the Jackson Laboratory and she grew curious again about what went on there. She applied for a job as an animal caretaker.

"When I was in school I was never very interested in science or scientific research," she admitted. "But I became fascinated with the work that is being done at the laboratory. The animals, I learned, are interesting in themselves. But, more than that, I learned that I was taking part in some of the most important research in the country."

For more than half a century, other people have

been curious about the laboratory's work, and surprised and excited when they discovered its importance. The laboratory was founded in 1929 by Clarence Cook Little. He had been president of the Universities of Maine and Michigan, but one of his chief interests was research on the causes and possible cures of cancer. He was among the first scientists to realize how useful a tool mice could be in the study of that disease.

Other scientists had used mice in their experiments. Dr. Little, however, improved on this idea. He became interested in the new science of genetics, which tries to explain how characteristics such as physical features, or even diseases and defects, are passed on from parents to their children.

Dr. Little decided to make use of the new science. He believed that scientists would be able to produce better results if all the animals in any single experiment were identical. At that time, the results of many experiments on animals were puzzling because the animals had different characteristics to begin with.

Dr. Little changed all this. He created an "inbred strain" of mice. He did this by mating the siblings—or brothers and sisters—from the same litter. After many generations of such matings, all the mice in this strain were as alike as identical twins.

Until this time, scientists believed that the matings between siblings from any species of mammals were harmful. Whatever defects the parents had would be passed on to the young. Dr. Little agreed, but that did not bother him. He *wanted* the defects—such as a ten-

Jax Mice have convenient feeding trays and water bottles in their cages.

dency toward certain diseases—to be passed on from one generation to another in some of his strains of mice. In that way, he hoped to be able to study and understand the defects.

Dr. Little interested several wealthy men and women in his plans. These people spent their summer vacations in Bar Harbor, a town that lies on a beautiful island of forests and mountains along the Maine Coast. Dr. Little had been coming to that area for many years to study the local plants and animals with his students. He opened a laboratory there in 1929 and named it for Roscoe B. Jackson, an automobile manufacturer who had helped Little to fulfill his plans.

The most valuable property of the Jackson Laboratory was a colony of inbred mice that Dr. Little had developed in 1909 when he was still a college student. Other strains of mice were soon added to the laboratory's stocks. Although Dr. Little had difficulty finding money to keep his laboratory open, a small number of scientists recognized the possibilities for carrying on original research there.

Dr. Little made a wise decision at the very beginning. He believed in women's rights to equal opportunity in a period when women scientists rarely were given a chance to carry on important research. Since that time, women scientists have fully participated in the projects at the laboratory and worked on an equal footing with their male colleagues.

At first, the people of Bar Harbor did not know what to make of the new laboratory. As they traveled past it, they caught a strong odor of the mice that were being raised in the primitive buildings. Someone started a rumor that the laboratory was going to be closed, and all of the mice would then be turned loose. Some people thought the mice might cause a plague.

But soon the Jackson Laboratory was accepted by the townspeople. Some of them went to work there. The scientists who moved to Bar Harbor from other parts of the country became a respected part of the community.

As the laboratory's programs expanded during the hard times that came with the Great Depression, Dr. Little struggled to find enough money to keep his laboratory going. His mice reproduced quickly and soon more mice were available than the scientists there needed for their research.

But the many exciting discoveries they were making convinced researchers in other laboratories that the inbred mice from the Jackson Laboratory were more useful than the animals they assembled for their own experiments. Larger experimental animals, such as rabbits, cats, and dogs, do not breed as often as mice do, and they are not as easy to care for in a laboratory. Dr. Little began to sell his extra mice to institutions in other parts of the country.

The demand for Jax Mice grew quickly. During World War II, the Federal Government bought thousands of mice every week for research on the tropical diseases that threatened American servicemen. The Jackson Laboratory was producing mice as well as studying them.

Then, in 1947, disaster struck. A great fire, fanned by high winds, swept the eastern part of Mount Desert Island. The forests burned and many of the big summer homes of wealthy vacationers were destroyed. The Jackson Laboratory caught fire and its stocks—or strains—of valuable mice died in the flames.

The world's scientific community came to the rescue. Jax Mice had been sent to hundreds of laboratories, hospitals, and universities. When news of the fire reached those institutions, their scientists offered to send back strains of mice they had received from Bar Harbor. In that way, the laboratory would be able to rebuild its colonies with the direct descendants of inbred mice that had originated there.

"The day after the fire, offers to send mice began to come in," wrote Jean Holstein in her book, *The First Fifty Years at the Jackson Laboratory.* "Some arrived within a week or two, and one lot that came back had not been out of the original Jax shipping box. Reaching their destination at the same time as news of the disaster, they were promptly shipped back. More than fifty individuals and institutions returned mice, including the second grade of the Whipple School in North Troy, N.Y. Eventually all but one of the stocks maintained before the fire were returned."

A new, fireproof laboratory rose from the ashes. The colonies of Jax Mice were restored to their former numbers, and then they went on growing. The descendants of the inbred strain developed by Clarence Cook Little in 1909 have multiplied and spread to hundreds of research institutions. At the Jackson Laboratory, researchers use more than 800,000 inbred mice in their experiments each year. Another two million Jax Mice are shipped by truck and air to places as far away as France, Australia, Japan, and the Soviet Union.

When Susan Grindle walked past the Jackson Laboratory during her girlhood, she used to imagine thousands of mice scampering all over the building. After she went to work there, she formed a far different picture. She learned that it takes a great deal of care and attention to raise nearly three million mice. Each mouse is carefully examined not once but several times. The scientists and caretakers keep track of every animal—its whereabouts, its state of health, and even its ancestry—from the moment it is born until it dies or leaves the laboratory.

"If we make a mistake in the mouse-breeding rooms, we might cause scientists to lose valuable time in their research," Susan Grindle said. "We have to make certain that we fill out our records correctly and that we don't get mice into the wrong cages. We must pay attention all the time we are handling the mice."

Without this attention to detail from the very beginning, the animals that come from the lab would not truly be Jax Mice.

3 · The Clean Barrier

An engine roared as a fork-lift truck rolled through the open doorway into the building. Small dollies—or pushcarts—clattered across the room's concrete floor. The heavy door of a machine that looked like a giant-sized pressure cooker clanged shut. The noise and the activity made this part of the building seem not at all like a laboratory where delicate medical research takes place.

"This building, where we raise most of our mice, is divided into three areas," Dr. Edwin P. Les explained to the man and woman who had come to visit the Jackson Laboratory. "We call one the Clean Supply Area. The others are the Washing Area, and finally the mouse rooms."

Dr. Les is the Supervisor of Research and Development. He is an energetic man of medium height, with eyeglasses and a tuft of gray beard. He seems constantly on the move, his sharp eyes picking out everything that is going on around him, and he often speaks of what he sees with a sense of humor. As he looked around him now, he saw the heap of soiled clothes on a rack against the wall, the spot of oil left on the floor by a truck, and a box of trash waiting to be removed.

"Obviously," he said, "we are not in the Clean Supply Area."

Disease is the reason for the Jackson Laboratory's existence. The laboratory was founded to discover the causes of disease in human beings, and to find ways to cure them. But mice, too, are subject to many diseases that may kill them or leave them unfit for use by scientists. The Jackson Laboratory has gone to great lengths to keep its mice healthy.

"Our first line of defense here is a barrier system against disease," Dr. Les said. "This room is where it all starts. All the supplies for the mouse colonies are brought here and stored. And beyond that wall over there is the Clean Supply Area. Everything—feed, bedding, even the clothes that the workers wear in there—must be treated so that they cannot contaminate the mice."

Two workers in the storage area pushed a dolly across the room. It was piled with large paper bags that held mouse feed. One of the men opened the metal door of the big "pressure cooker" and pushed in the bags of feed. Then he closed the door.

"Those machines are called autoclaves," Dr. Les said. "They are steam chambers that disinfect all the materials we use. The mouse feed is pasteurized in there, just as the milk you drink has been pasteurized by a heating process to kill bacteria and other harmful organisms."

A worker closes the heavy metal door of the autoclave. Inside, steam disinfects food, bedding, and other material for the cages.

Dr. Les led his visitors to a large window where they could look into the Clean Supply Area. This was a busy place, too. Workers opened the autoclave doors to remove the bags of feed that had already passed through and been pasteurized. A worker lifted a bag, shook it vigorously to loosen any feed inside that might have stuck together in the steam, and dropped it on a dolly. From there the feed would go to the mouse rooms.

"Those big bags that are coming out of the other autoclave hold the wood shavings that we use for bedding," Dr. Les pointed out. "They are shavings from white pine boards. We buy the shavings from a lum-

Wood shavings come to the lab in large paper bags. After they are disinfected, they are measured into the clean cages by a mechanical dispenser.

ber mill near here. The boards generally are stacked outdoors for a time, and there is a chance that they have been soiled by wild mice or birds. So we have to disinfect them, too. The bags are emptied into that big dispenser over there, and measured out into the mouse cages."

Inside the Clean Supply Area, other men and women were busy preparing various materials for the mouse rooms. Cages that had been changed by the animal caretakers were coming back into the area through tunnel washers, where they had been cleaned with hot detergents, rinsed, and dried with hot air. Water bottles were coming from a second washing machine, while drinking tubes and rubber stoppers for the bottles were passing through still another machine.

"The mouse feed is prepared for us from a special recipe by a company in Connecticut," Dr. Les said. "There are ten different recipes, and each strain of mice is routinely fed only one of them. They contain wheat, skim milk, fish meal, soybean meal, oats, alfalfa, and lots of other things. The feed is also shipped to us with extra vitamins in it because some of the nourishment is lost when it is pasteurized.

"Water for the mice is treated with a small amount of hydrochloric acid pumped from those huge glass bottles over there," he went on. "We put some vitamins in the water, too. The acid kills a certain kind of bacteria that is harmful to mice."

One of Dr. Les's visitors pointed to two young men in the Clean Supply Area and asked who they

The water bottles are thoroughly washed and rinsed before going back to the cages. Each one is fitted with a rubber stopper and a drinking tube.

were. Both men were dressed in plain white coveralls and wore light plastic "booties" over their feet.

"Those are scientists visiting here from Asia," Dr. Les answered. "Ordinarily, visitors are not allowed into the Clean Supply Area or the mouse rooms. The people who come on some kind of business are permitted past the barrier, but they must wash their hands and arms and change into clothing that has been disinfected."

The visitors remarked on the strict regulations that have been set up at the Jackson Laboratory to protect the mice against disease and contamination. As Dr. Les recounted the laboratory's history, however, they gained a better understanding of the need for security.

There was a sudden demand for inbred strains of mice after World War II. The National Institutes of Health needed large numbers of mice for experiments with drugs that were thought to be effective against cancer. The government ordered the mice from the Jackson Laboratory, but the laboratory did not have enough to fill the order. It was still rebuilding after the great fire and there was not enough room to raise all the mice that the government needed.

The laboratory's scientists began a frantic search for nearby buildings that could be used to house more mice.

"They went out and bought or rented every suitable building in Bar Harbor and nearby towns that they could find," Dr. Les recalled. "They fitted up an old dance hall as a mouse house. They also rented an abandoned funeral home and put mice in there, too."

But large colonies of animals that are confined in a small space are subject to diseases and other hazards. Epidemics often sweep through such colonies and destroy them. Somehow, harmful organisms such as bacteria and parasites got into the mouse colonies. Although most of the mice survived, they were not as healthy as scientists wanted them to be.

When more space became available at the laboratory itself, the old buildings were shut down. The mice colonies were moved to the new quarters where they could be watched more effectively.

Mice, living closely together, are subject to many diseases. Scientists carefully prepare their water, using these machines and giant bottles, to protect the animals' health.

"The laboratory's scientists began what they called a 'test and slaughter program,'" Dr. Les said. "Every mouse was examined before it was allowed into the new mouse rooms. If it passed two successive tests, the scientists found a place for it. If it showed signs of disease, it was killed humanely with chloroform.

"But it turned out that many of the mice in the laboratory were only 'semiclean.' Some of them carried parasites such as lice and mites in their fur and pinworms in their intestines. The people here tried very hard to get rid of the parasites. They dipped the mice in various chemicals. One scientist claimed that he had a sure cure by making a mixture of sulfur and gasoline. He dipped his mice in it—and all their hair fell out!"

Dr. Les had been a graduate student at Ohio State University. He did his research there under the direction of Dr. Earl L. Green. Dr. Green was interested in genetics and cancer research and kept a colony of his own mice at Ohio State. When Clarence Cook Little retired in 1956, Dr. Green was appointed the laboratory's new director.

"I had been helping Dr. Green at Ohio State, testing the effects of small amounts of radiation on mice," Dr. Les said. "He told me he would not be able to carry on this research, along with his duties at the Jackson Laboratory, unless I joined him there as a research assistant. My first job was to bring Dr. Green's mice to Bar Harbor. I rented a truck and drove east from Ohio with 400 mice. It took me three days to reach Bar Harbor."

Some scientists, such as Dr. Green, bring their own colonies of mice when they join the staff of the Jackson Laboratory. Sometimes scientists there order mice of a new strain that has been discovered at another institution. To protect its own supply of mice, the staff at Jackson Laboratory has always carefully observed mice that arrive from other places before adding them to its own colonies. Imported mice often bring new diseases into a laboratory. One of the ways to test new mice is to put some of the laboratory's own mice into a cage in direct contact with them. If the "contact" mice sicken or die, then the staff knows that the new mice are diseased.

"We put some Jax Mice in with Dr. Green's mice," Dr. Les recalled. "And, do you know what happened? Dr. Green's mice got sick! It turned out that his colony was healthier than the one here at the laboratory."

The new director acted forcefully to create one of the cleanest mouse colonies in the world at the Jackson Laboratory. New measures were taken, as we shall see, to rid the colony of diseases caused by parasites, viruses, and bacteria. New regulations were put into effect to try to make certain that whatever enters the mouse rooms—materials and mice, or men and women —does not carry contamination in, too.

This is the atmosphere in which the animal caretakers go about their daily work.

4 · The Animal Caretaker

Karla Reed is an animal caretaker in one of the mouse-breeding rooms at the Jackson Laboratory. She was married just after leaving high school and this is the first full-time job she has ever had. She arrives at the lab at seven-thirty every weekday morning. Before she enters the mouse room, she must pass through the "clean barrier."

Along one side of the building there is a row of doors that enter directly into small rooms called "locks." Some locks are for women, others for men. When Karla Reed enters the lock, she removes her shoes and street clothes and hangs them against the wall.

Then she climbs over a low barrier in the middle of the lock. On the other side, after carefully washing her hands and arms with disinfectant soap, she finds the disinfected uniform that the laboratory provides for those who work with mice. (Women caretakers have a choice between a laboratory dress and slacks-and-blouse.) She also puts on a pair of shoes that she bought with a cash allowance from the laboratory. Although she owns the shoes, they never leave the mouse room area. Then she goes straight from the lock to a basin in the mouse room where she again washes her hands and arms with disinfectant soap.

"The first thing you learn when you come to work here is to change your clothes about eight times a day, and to wash your hands about five hundred times," she laughed. "Any time we leave the mouse room area, whether it is for lunch or one of our coffee breaks, we go through this whole process. We leave our lab clothes on the mouse room side, and put on our street clothes on the outdoor side. Then we reverse the process when we come back in."

Like the other eighty or more animal caretakers who work in the mouse-breeding rooms or in the research labs, Karla Reed received her training on the job. She learned to handle the mice by going into the mouse rooms and working alongside one of the room leaders. But she had a head start on most of the other new caretakers.

"I kept mice when I was a girl," she said. "I grew up on a small island off Bar Harbor, and every once in a while I would rescue a wild mouse that had been injured by a cat and nurse it back to health. Later on somebody gave me some pet white mice."

The laboratory asks the animal caretakers not to keep mice, gerbils, hamsters, guinea pigs, and other rodents as pets. There is a possibility that anyone who handles such pets at home might accidentally carry parasites or diseases with them into the mouse rooms. But Karla Reed no longer has to entertain herself with one or two mice at home. When she enters the breeding room, she is surrounded by 4,800 cages of them. Every day she and the other caretakers in the room must each transfer the mice from about 300 soiled cages into clean ones.

The breeding cages, like almost everything else at the Jackson Laboratory, have changed over the years.

A caretaker cleans the floors, walls, and other surfaces of the room. Each of them cares for 4,800 cages of mice.

Right from the start, they were divided into two compartments so that more mice could be handled in the space of a day. The cages were made of wooden boxes for many years, but the mice were always gnawing holes in them in an attempt to escape.

The wooden boxes were replaced by stainless-steel cages, which proved easier to keep clean. Now they, in turn, are being replaced by clear plastic cages. The caretakers are able to watch the mice through the plastic sides. A hood of synthetic fabric over the top keeps out dust or bits of fur from the cages above.

Changing 300 cages a day is time-consuming but interesting work. Each strain of mice seems to behave differently.

"Some strains are very gentle, almost like pets," Karla Reed said. "Others are like finely bred race-horses. They're very jumpy and active, and they tend to make some of the caretakers nervous, too. And one or two of the strains are just plain mean. The males really tear up the females and the pups, and sometimes they hurt them badly or kill them."

The mice react not only to each other, but to the caretakers as well. If a caretaker is nervous, or even afraid, in the presence of some strains of mice, they will become aggressive and more difficult to handle. Some mice, ordinarily gentle, may react suddenly in a completely new way. Perhaps they are set off by the odor of someone's perfume or hair spray, or perhaps an approaching storm outside has made them jittery.

Some of the caretakers' duties amount to simple "housekeeping." They clean the floors, walls, and other surfaces of the room. They change the mice to fresh cages, fill the hopper with feed, and put the soiled cages into the locks where they will be picked up by other workers for washing before going back to the Clean Supply Area.

But the most interesting work occurs while the mice are being transferred to fresh cages. Karla Reed has learned to work swiftly and surely over each cage. Taking a pair of long forceps from the disinfectant jar, she reaches into the cage and picks up a mouse by the middle of its tail. (If she grasped the tail by the tip, a nervous mouse would have more freedom to flip back and perhaps nip her hand.) When she lifts the mouse from the cage, she notes its sex and its physical condition before putting it into its new home.

"They go into a fresh cage every week, and it's always interesting to watch their reactions," she said. "Right away they become very busy exploring the wood shavings. They're not satisfied until they've gone over every inch of them two or three times. They want to get familiar with their new surroundings."

There are often great changes in a cage from one week to the next. The female may have given birth to a litter of pups since the last time the caretaker looked in on her. The birth may have taken place several days earlier. If so, the caretaker must be able to determine the exact age of the young so that accurate records can be kept.

"The first day the pups are red all over," Karla Reed explained. "They have no hair at all, and their skin is very thin and transparent. When they are one

The mice are put into a fresh cage every week.

day old, they have been nursing for a while and you can see a plain white spot around their belly right through their skin. That's the milk they've been drinking.

"They are a little lighter in color the second day," she went on. "Their ears are still stuck close to the head like tiny doorknobs. The ears begin to grow out from the head, and when they are four days old the ears are strong and held straight back.

Some mice pups and their mother.

"By the fifth day the skin is getting lighter and it is much thicker, almost like rubber. When the pups are six days old a little fuzz begins to sprout on the back of the neck. There is a coat of light fuzz all over them when they are seven days old. If they are white mice, it looks as if they've been dipped in a snowbank."

The mice grow quickly. ("I like them best when they are three weeks old because then they are all fat and fuzzy," Karla Reed said.) Most of the mice remain in the breeding cage until they are about four weeks old. Then they are sent to a new home—either to a research laboratory there in Bar Harbor or to a new laboratory that may be as far away as Asia or Africa.

A few of the pups are removed earlier. A sharp-eyed caretaker may detect something odd about a young mouse. The oddity may be as obvious as a pair of useless hind legs. Or it may be as slight as a droopy ear, or a white patch of fur on the pup's back. In any case, the caretaker fills out a card on the "deviant mouse" and reports it to the supervisor.

"It keeps us on our toes," Karla Reed said. "If your name is on the card and the mouse turns out to be something really special, you will get credit for finding it. It's part of the excitement of working here."

As Karla Reed said, everyone must be alert for surprises around these mice. They are among the most remarkable animals in the world.

5 · The House Mouse

Scientists who studied the remains of early civilizations in the Middle East discovered mousetraps that had been made of baked clay. This find, and the appearance of the bones of mice in ancient buildings, suggest that mice adopted human beings long before we decided they could be useful to us, too.

The house mouse is well named. Although most wild animals are afraid of us and stay as far away from us as possible, the house mouse moved right in with us very early in our history. This tendency to make use of our homes and our food—as well as bits of our clothing for nesting material—gives the house mouse an advantage over its fellow wild creatures in the modern world. While we have destroyed the wilderness homes of many animals, we have gone on putting up buildings for ourselves—and, of course, for the house mouse.

The house mouse did very well for untold centuries before humans came on the scene. It is a member of the most successful of all the orders of mammals, the rodents. This order includes many kinds of mice, in addition to rats, squirrels, hamsters, gerbils,

The house mouse was considered an enemy by our ancestors. Now it is important to our well-being.

woodchucks, porcupines, and prairie dogs. Although its largest member, the beaver, is about two and a half feet long, most rodents are small animals. They all have four prominent incisors, or chisel-like teeth, in the front of their mouths which they use for gnawing.

The natural food of rodents is mainly vegetable matter, such as seeds and nuts. As a rule, these animals keep to their wild ways and do us no harm. In fact, we are hardly aware of the presence of the hundreds of different kinds of rodents in our world. A few of them are considered pests when they eat our vegetables, as woodchucks sometimes do, or strip the bark off our trees, as porcupines sometimes do. But several kinds of rats and mice have attached themselves so closely to our homes and farms that we almost always consider them serious pests. The house mouse, which scientists call *Mus musculus*, is the most widespread of these "constant companions."

The house mouse apparently was attracted to human settlements soon after our ancestors gave up the wandering life of the hunter and began to cultivate crops. In the wild, this animal feeds largely on the seeds of grasses. All of our grain crops are descended from wild grasses, and the fields of wheat and other domesticated crops attracted the house mouse. Soon this animal, which is very curious about its surroundings, discovered that humans even harvested the grain for it and stored the crop conveniently in nice little piles in their houses. The house mouse, which is small and not easily noticed, moved right in.

Many scientists believe that the house mouse originated in the dry highlands of central Asia. But once it learned that humans were a source of food, it spread across Asia and into North Africa and southern Europe. Then, as humans spread across the globe from those regions, the house mouse followed them. It traveled, as our ancestors did, by ship across the oceans to the Americas, Australia, and even remote oceanic islands. Today it moves almost as easily by air, hidden in the cargo aboard planes.

When our ancestors learned that the house mouse took a good part of their carefully grown crops for itself, they did everything they could to rid themselves of this tiny pest. They learned to keep cats, which ate many mice. (In ancient Egypt, the people considered the cat to be a god. Among other things, they admired its skill at catching these pests.) In other places the angry farmers invented mousetraps, or burned the stacks of litter in which mice built their nests.

But the house mouse had been living with enemies long before humans turned against them. Hundreds of birds and mammals hunt mice for food. Hawks and owls, as well as weasels, foxes, wolves, bears, skunks, and various kinds of wild cats are among the predators that depend heavily on mice for their living. But the house mouse has gone right on thriving. Only within the last hundred years or so have we discovered that many of the qualities that make the house mouse such a successful pest also make it valuable in the struggle against human disease.

The house mouse is familiar to almost everybody, either through pictures or personal experience. It has a pointed snout, whiskers, large ears, and small eyes. The nose constantly twitches, trying to detect smells nearby, and the ears are alert for every sound. A mouse depends on the nose and mouth to tell it what is going on nearby, because its eyes are of little use in making out objects more than two inches away. Those beady little eyes are, in truth, extremely nearsighted.

The body of the house mouse, including the head, is three or four inches long. Its scaly tail is about as long as its body. People usually believe that the tail is "naked," but on close inspection it is seen to be lightly covered with short hairs.

In the wild, the fur of the house mouse is almost always grayish brown, with a hint of yellow. When we speak of some object as being "mousy," we are referring not only to its color tone, but also to a kind of insignificant appearance.

But the animal's coloring, like its small size and weight, has contributed to its success. The little creature usually passes in and out of our houses unnoticed. It hides in the smallest places and squeezes through the narrowest chinks. It is so light, weighing only about an ounce, that it travels in our boxes and packages without being detected.

The house mouse faces many hazards. Animals of all kinds hunt it. Human beings try to rid their homes and storehouses of it. Drought and other natural disasters can wipe out much of its food supply. Diseases of many types affect its colonies.

Yet the house mouse is always with us. It is extremely prolific—which means that it produces many offspring. It mates often, perhaps five to ten times a year in different situations. Each time it may give birth to six or more young. If it can escape disease and predators, it may live to be two years old, or more.

The house mouse tends to live in small, closely related groups. Scientists have pointed out that most living things, including human beings, generally seek their mates outside the family group. If they interbreed with closely related individuals, they are likely to keep passing on harmful characteristics to their offspring. But the house mouse often mates with its brothers or sisters.

Some ancient people, particularly in China and Japan, kept mice as pets. They noticed that dramatic changes often took place within a single family of house mice. One of a litter of the grayish brown animals suddenly would turn out to grow fur of an entirely different color. Perhaps a mouse would be born pure white. Or perhaps it would be spotted black and white, or have pink eyes.

There were other strange mice born among an otherwise normal litter. The Japanese discovered that occasionally a house mouse ran around in circles, reminding them of a person dancing. These animals eventually were called "dancing mice."

Both the Japanese and the Chinese became collectors of "fancy mice"—those animals that showed unusual colors or behavior. For many centuries, no one undersood how the different traits came about. People knew nothing about genes, or the ways in which certain traits were passed on to offspring. But they knew enough to breed fancy mice by mating them with each other. By mating two white mice, for instance, they were able to produce the large numbers of white mice they wanted.

The hobby of collecting fancy mice spread to Europe, and later to the United States. Collectors learned to breed different types of the house mice, just as gardeners learned to grow different kinds of roses or apples. By keeping their mice breeding within closely related groups—by keeping them inbred—the collectors maintained the qualities that made them "fancy."

Yet, even so, sometimes a different kind of mouse appeared suddenly in these inbred colonies. A mouse might grow fur of a different color than its parents, or be born with a crooked tail, or be able to scamper only in circles.

As we shall see in Chapter 7, it was not until around the year 1900 that scientists began to understand the reasons for these sudden changes within a family of mice or other animals. Shortly after that, Clarence Cook Little bought the fancy mice that were to become the basis for several inbred strains in the huge collection of Jax Mice.

Collectors learned to breed different types of house mice: black, white, and streaked or spotted.

6 · The Mutant Mart

Four staff members, wearing white laboratory coats, met in the hallway above the mouse-breeding rooms at the Jackson Laboratory.

"Well, let's see what they have collected for us this morning," one of the women said.

Dr. Muriel Davisson and three professional assistants, Hope Sweet, Sally Fox, and Janice Southard, walked into a small room off the hallway. Most of the room was occupied by a long metal table. Standing on the table were a dozen or so round cardboard boxes that looked like quart-sized ice cream containers. Each of the boxes had air holes punched in the cover. A curious sound, as if something were rustling around inside, could be heard coming from the boxes.

This room is jokingly called the "Mutant Mart." Every Tuesday morning the animal caretakers set aside the pups that seem to have some unusual characteristic. They are put in the small boxes and sent to this room. Scientists come there from the different research laboratories in the other buildings in the hope of discovering an unusual characteristic that may lead to a new strain of mice.

Scientists gather at the "Mutant Mart" once a week to look for mice with rare traits. If they find one, it may help them solve an age-old medical mystery.

Hope Sweet took the forceps from a disinfectant jar on the table, removed the cover from the first box, and looked inside. Then she lifted a small mouse from the shavings in the bottom of the box and set it on the table. The mouse, which was less than three weeks old, carefully explored the tabletop.

"It's a pretty little thing," Hope Sweet said, pointing with the forceps to the mouse's head. "See, it has a white spot on its muzzle."

The others gathered around her for a closer look

at the little mouse. Aside from the white blaze near the nose, the mouse was a plain grayish brown and seemed normal in every respect.

"I've seen that little white spot on other young mice," Hope Sweet told the others, "and so I know it is not something that is inherited. I've tried to mate mice like that, but none of its offspring or descendants will have the white nose. It's just that every once in a while it will show up in a mouse."

"It may be because there is some defect in the pigment in that spot that prevents the color from coming in," Sally Fox explained to a visitor. "For instance, its mother might have nipped it accidentally when she was grooming it, and the fur came in differently there."

Hope Sweet put the mouse back in the box and moved off down the side of the table. The little mouse was not the kind of thing she and the other scientists were looking for. They began to open the other boxes.

Most of the time they find nothing out of the ordinary. Skillful and experienced, these scientists are able to tell after a brief examination whether the "unusual" mouse is of any special interest to them. The animal may simply be sick or injured, and in that case it will be humanely destroyed.

Mutant comes from the Latin word *mutare*, meaning "to change." A *mutant* is an animal that is born with some trait or characteristic that sets it apart from the other members of its family. This unusual trait is caused by a sudden change in one of its genes, the elements that determine the traits that every living thing inherits from its parents.

If the scientists discover an animal that seems to be a mutant, they will take it to a research laboratory and try to find out the cause of its unusual trait. Is this trait just the result of an injury or sickness after all? Or is it caused by a change in one of the animal's genes? If so, can the scientists mate that animal with another one so that this change is passed on to its descendants? If that happens, a new mutant mouse will be added to the colonies of Jax Mice so that it may help in future medical research.

The development of such a valuable research animal begins when a sharp-eyed animal caretaker notices something unusual about a young mouse. The second step takes place here in the Mutant Mart. Trained scientists examine each of these animals and determine which ones show promise of some important discovery.

"The card that the animal caretaker filled out says this mouse drags its hind legs," Hope Sweet said to the visitor as she opened another box and lifted out the animal. "We always look closely at a mouse like this, because it may be suffering from some condition similar to muscular dystrophy in humans."

She put the mouse on the table. One of the hind legs was almost normal, but the other hung limply by the animal's side.

"It could have a back injury," Sally Fox suggested.

"Yes," Dr. Davisson agreed. "Some strains of mice are more likely to receive back injuries than others. It often happens to very nervous strains. They may hurt themselves in the cage. Or an inexperienced caretaker may jab it in the back with the forceps while trying to pick it up."

"Even if it is a genetic condition, I probably wouldn't take this one," Hope Sweet said. "Jan is working with dystrophic mice in her laboratory. If I were going to study it I would have to get mice from her to mate with this one, so I'll just leave it for her."

Janice Southard walked around the table to look at the mouse. She held the animal by the tail with her forceps and watched the way it moved.

"This mouse looks pretty healthy," she said. "A dystrophic mouse is all hunched over. It may simply be that this mouse is very young and for some reason—overcrowded in a large litter, perhaps—it hasn't used its legs enough yet. I don't think there is anything very special here."

The scientists continued to open the boxes and look inside. In one box there was a runt in a litter with eleven siblings.

"No wonder it's tiny!" Sally Fox said. "With that mob, it probably isn't getting enough to eat."

"It looks like that mouse needs some love mash," Janice Southard said, and everybody laughed.

"Some of us make up special recipes to feed the mice that we work with in our own research laboratories," Hope Sweet explained. "For instance, in one research laboratory we have a special strain of mice from Asia. They don't do so well on the ordinary diet that Jax Mice get, so the workers in the mouse room give their mice rice as a supplement. We also make up

Some mice are very small, or have other traits that distinguish them from their brothers and sisters.

a dish like granola that we call 'love mash.' Most of the mice really go for it. But some mice don't like the smell when we add cod liver oil to their love mash."

"Yes," laughed Sally Fox. "They keep burying it in their wood shavings!"

The scientists examined a black mouse that had only one eye. They agreed that the mouse was from an inbred strain in which this condition occurred with great regularity.

"Almost 10 percent of the young animals in this strain have only one eye," Dr. Davisson said. "It's not unusual, and we even sell them along with their normal brothers and sisters to other institutions for general research work. Everybody expects a few one-eyed mice from this strain and it doesn't affect working with them."

There was a litter of young mice in a box at the

end of the table. At first glance, all the mice looked very much alike. But when Hope Sweet held up one of them, everybody could see that its fur was colored a darker brown than that of its brothers and sisters. Its eyes were a pinkish red, while the others' were dark.

"This one could be a mutant," Hope Sweet explained to the visitor. "There might be a new gene here that affects the animal's color. We'll take this one back to our research lab. We'll mate it with another animal that looks something like it and see if we can reproduce this coloring in its descendants. If it can pass on these traits—the special color of its fur and the pinkish-red eyes—we will know that it is a true mutant."

Back in their research laboratories, these scientists will be making use of genetics, one of the most exciting branches of modern science. *Genetics* is the study of how all living things pass on characteristics—such as the color of their eyes, the shape of their ears, or even serious defects and diseases—to their offspring. Genetics also tries to explain how *mutations*, sudden changes, occur in a plant or an animal, including human beings.

More than 400 mutant mice have been collected at the Jackson Laboratory. Scientists, using their skill and imagination, are studying these unusual animals in an attempt to tell us more about ourselves.

7 · Heredity

People made use of the principles of heredity for thousands of years without truly understanding them. Whenever a gardener crossed two kinds of apple trees to produce a tastier apple, or a sportsman mated two kinds of horses to develop a racing champion, that person was putting genetics to work.

There were limits on how much could be accomplished, however. No one had ever figured out how various physical traits—such as tastiness in apples, or running speed in horses—are passed down from one generation to another.

The first man to do so was an Austrian monk named Gregor Mendel. Mendel liked to experiment with plants in his monastery garden. He produced *hybrids*, which are the offspring of two different kinds of parents.

In 1866 Mendel published a paper about his experiments. He described his theory of how the pea plants in his garden transmitted the tallness or shortness of their stems, and the smoothness or roughness of the pea shells, to new generations of plants. Mendel's paper went almost unnoticed. No one recognized its importance until thirty-five years later, when trained scientists began to unravel the same mystery.

This is what Mendel discovered. When he crossed tall pea plants with short ones, all of the offspring turned out to be tall. This result puzzled him at first. But the short plants reappeared in the second generation of hybrids, when about one out of every four plants had a short stem.

Mendel discovered that when two different kinds of plants are crossed, each seems to pass on its own characteristics to later generations. But some characteristics, he decided, are always "dominant" over oth-

Scientists at the Jackson Laboratory work with different traits of the house mouse, just as Gregor Mendel worked with different kinds of plants.

ers. For instance, in pea plants, tallness is dominant over shortness.

But just because all of the plants in the first generation have tall stems, it does not mean that the hereditary material for shortness has disappeared. Mendel described this characteristic as "recessive." He discovered that this recessive characteristic may disappear in the first generation of hybrids, but it will make itself known again in the second generation. He knew that about one in four of these plants would be short, but he could not fully explain his results.

By careful observation and the use of mathematics, Mendel founded the science of genetics. Although modern scientists have cleared up further mysteries about how traits are passed on to new generations, Gregor Mendel worked out the basic pathways in his monastery garden. Those pathways are put to use in the production of Jax Mice.

Scientists now know more about the physical elements through which parents transmit their characteristics. They call these elements *genes*. Every living thing, plant or animal, carries two genes in its cells for each of its characteristics. Each pair of genes determines how some part of the organism's body will be shaped, or will behave.

There are more variations to the process than Mendel realized, but modern scientists understand it well enough to conduct complicated experiments using genetics. They try to trace the history of a gene as it is sent from a plant or an animal to its descendant.

Each parent contributes only one gene for a

Scientists at the lab are able to work out on paper the genetic lines that cause mice to show different traits.

characteristic to its offspring. The offspring, then, carries two genes for this characteristic, one from its father and the other from its mother. If the genes for this characteristic are the same in both parents, the offspring will be identical to them in this respect. This happens in the inbred strains of Jax Mice, where all the animals are as alike as identical twins.

But in most matings between plants or animals, each parent will pass on a number of different pairs of genes to the offspring. If the gene passed on by the father for a specific characteristic is different from that of the mother, one of the two genes will prove to be dominant. Let us say that a scientist at the Jackson Laboratory mates a dark mouse with a white mouse. Each of these two mice contributes a gene to its off-spring that determines color.

If the gene for dark fur is dominant, all of the offspring will be dark, though each will carry a *recessive* gene for their white fur. Then, if two of those offspring are mated, and produce four pups of their own, one of the pups is likely to have white fur. This mixture is a result of simple mathematics.

Here is how it works: There are four ways in which the genes may be combined in a pup of this second generation.

1. Each of the parents may transmit to the pup a gene for dark fur. This pup, of course, will have dark fur.
2. The father may transmit to the pup a gene for dark fur, and the mother a gene for white fur. Because the dark gene is dominant, the pup will have dark fur.
3. The mother may transmit to the pup a gene for dark fur, and the father a gene for white fur. Again, because the dark gene is dominant, the pup will have dark fur.
4. Each of the parents may transmit to the pup the recessive gene for white fur. But now, because this pup has no gene at all for dark color, its fur will be white. And if this pup is mated with

another white mouse, they will start a strain of mice with pure white fur.

The outcome of these matings is not always so exact. But the mathematical formula that Gregor Mendel worked out more than a hundred years ago is still useful. On the average, the recessive gene for a characteristic will make itself known in the second generation once in every four offspring.

Every once in a while an "accident" occurs. A gene that determines color may somehow be changed or damaged. A mouse, instead of having pure white fur, may be born with brown spots. The mutant gene may be recessive. But even so, it will reappear among the "grandchildren" of this mouse, when one of them will be born with spotted fur.

But scientists at the Jackson Laboratory want to preserve these mutants. They never know when a mouse with new characteristics may prove useful in their research.

"When mutants occur, we want to preserve them," said Priscilla Lane, the supervisor of the laboratory where mutant mice are kept. "We breed them here, and then we supply them to the world."

8 · Damaged Goods

We now know enough about the Jackson Laboratory to notice that its scientists have a curious attitude about "healthy" mice. On the one hand, they make a great effort to protect their animals against many diseases. On the other hand, they are excited by the discovery that certain mice are diseased or defective.

We might be inclined to think at first that there is some confusion in the laboratory's goals. It is only when we understand the difference between the *kinds* of disease that all the effort in the laboratory begins to make sense to us.

The scientists are always on guard against the spread of parasites, viruses, and other organisms that —like our own germs of the common cold—spread from one individual to another. A mouse colony that has been struck by a contagious disease is of little scientific interest. Scientists know how these diseases spread and what their effect will be on mice. Many of the animals die from the disease. Others will be weakened so that they are unfit for research purposes. These diseases are a threat to the entire colony because they spread so quickly.

But a mouse that is born with a hereditary disease or defect is of special interest. It did not "catch" the disease from other mice, nor can other mice in the colony "catch" the disease from it.

The defect or disease in this case is the result of a change in one of the animal's genes. A gene is not "catching." It can only be passed on to descendants when the affected mouse mates with another. The defect, or other new trait, can be acquired only through heredity.

Scientists at the Jackson Laboratory are interested in the science of heredity, which is called *genetics*. That is why they are excited by the discovery of a mutant—one of those animals that suddenly appears in the colony with a new trait that has been caused by a changed gene. An animal suffering from a contagious disease is of no use to scientists, and in fact could be harmful to the entire mouse colony.

A changed gene may not be harmful to an animal. It may simply produce a mouse with spotted fur, or a mouse with pink eyes. But sometimes the gene that determines an animal's physical appearance determines another characteristic as well. When this gene is changed or damaged, it could bring about changes in other parts of the animal's body besides its fur. It may change an element in the blood that makes the mouse anemic, or leaves it especially vulnerable to cancer.

By mating these mutants, scientists then will collect a supply of mice that have anemia or cancer. Because human beings also suffer from such diseases, mutant stocks of mice are valuable to researchers who are trying to understand and find a cure for them.

A valuable mutant at the Jackson Lab is the hairless mouse. The hairless mouse appeared like other mutants, quite by accident. A defect in a gene caused this condition in a pup that was born in an otherwise normal litter.

The strange thing about this mutant is that, at first, it does not look any different from normal pups. For the first ten days of its life it keeps on growing the expected coat of fur. Suddenly, something happens. The hair on its muzzle begins to fall out. Soon the entire head is hairless. Then the rest of the hair begins

Scientists at the lab are successful when they produce "damaged goods." This hairless mouse may carry a gene for leukemia and provide clues for curing the disease.

to fall out of its body, all the way back to its hind legs.

"At that point, the mouse is naked except for the hair on its hind legs," a scientist said. "It looks as if it is wearing a pair of fuzzy pants."

The hair disappears from the legs, too, and the mouse is completely "naked." The only hairs on its body are its whiskers! By breeding the first mutant at the laboratory with one of the hairless pups that appeared in a later generation, the staff has built up a stock of hairless mice.

The Jackson Laboratory sells many hairless mice. These mutants are valuable to institutions where tests on skin are carried out. As a rule, researchers who make skin tests must take the time to shave the animals for their experiments. In the case of the hairless mouse, a mutant gene has done this job for them.

Even more important to science was the discovery that hairless mice of a strain kept at Jackson Laboratory often have leukemia (not all strains of the mutant develop other harmful conditions). Doctors who study leukemia in humans also study hairless mice to learn more about the disease.

Some years ago, an animal caretaker at the Jackson Laboratory found a mouse with hind legs that were useless. The legs were weak and shriveled. Dr. Elizabeth Russell made a series of experiments that show the value of keeping records on every litter of mice born at the laboratory. She could not actually see the damaged gene. But she was able to trace it through the descendants of the original defective mouse because some of them were born with the same condition.

She knew then that the defect was the result of a mutant gene.

Other tests showed that the muscles in the hind legs of this mutant had deteriorated. Dr. Russell realized that this condition was very similar to muscular dystrophy, a mysterious disease that affects human beings. But to investigate the nature of the disease, many "dystrophic mice" would be needed. The trouble was that these mice were often too sick to breed and reproduce naturally.

Scientists at the laboratory solved the problem of producing the dystrophic mice they needed. They made use of the fact that, in most matings, all members of the litter in which a sick mouse occurred also carried a dystrophic gene. Because this gene was recessive in the siblings, however, they appeared to be normal.

How did the scientists know that the siblings of the sick mouse carried the defective gene, too? Again, record-keeping was important. When the normal-looking siblings of sick mice were later mated among themselves, a dystrophic mouse eventually appeared among their descendants. This event told the scientists that the gene was carried by the "family" even when its members appeared to be normal. These animals, then, could be used to produce large numbers of mice that showed all the symptoms of the disease. This is how it was done:

The scientists removed the ovaries from sick females and transplanted them to healthy females. Then they selected males that carried the recessive gene for dystrophy and mated them with the healthy females.

In this way, they collected large numbers of dystrophic mice.

The scientists carried out even more complicated matings with these mice. They took sperm from sick males who could not breed and implanted it in *healthy* females that carried the ovaries of the *sick* females. All the mice that were born from these matings carried two dystrophic genes. All of them had muscular dystrophy.

Although the cause of muscular dystrophy in human beings has not been found, much progress has been made through studies on dystrophic mice. These studies show that the disease is inherited through the mother. Doctors are now able to identify women who carry the defective genes.

Today the Jackson Laboratory houses a great variety of mutant mice. Some are dwarves. Others are hairless, obese, diabetic, or have some other unusual characteristic of color, structure, or behavior.

Each kind of mutant has been given a name that briefly, and often vividly, describes it. Here are some of the names of mutant stocks that are listed in the catalog that the Jackson Laboratory sends out to other institutions:

Balding, Bouncy, Broad-headed, Bent-tail, Curly-whiskers, Dancer, Droopy-ear, Fidget, Frizzy, Flaky-tail, Fuzzy, Frowsy, Greasy, Jerker, Jittery, Kinky, Motheaten, Pugnose, Pudgy, Shiverer, Trembly, Tumbler, Tubby, Twirler, Twitcher, Waddler, Waltzer, and Wobbler.

The names may be comical, but each of these

animals is part of a serious study. The mouse whose patchy fur looks "motheaten," or the mouse that wanders around in circles like a "waltzer," may someday provide the key to solving an age-old medical mystery.

9 · An Animal Doctor

Dr. Terrie Cunliffe-Beamer, a slender, light-haired woman, is a veterinarian at the Jackson Laboratory. She is one of the scientists who are responsible for keeping Jax Mice free from contaminants and contagious diseases.

"When I was in college and our professors needed fifty rats for an experiment, they always ordered seventy-five," she said. "They knew that in a couple of weeks they would have only fifty left anyway. A large number of them would die. There are many infections and parasites that affect animals when great numbers of them are confined close together."

The Jackson Laboratory could not exist if its colonies were weakened by such infections. They would be useless to the laboratory's research scientists and unwanted at other institutions. Yet keeping disease from the three million Jax Mice that are produced every year is an enormous and never-ending responsibility.

The public is generally familiar with two kinds of veterinarians. One kind is in private practice, treating house pets such as dogs and cats, and domestic animals

Dr. Terrie Cunliffe-Beamer, a veterinarian at the Jackson Laboratory.

on small farms. This veterinarian's job is to cure animals that are sick or injured.

The other kind of veterinarian is employed by large dairy farms, cattle growers, and chicken-and-egg producers. The concern there is generally preventive medicine. The job in that case is to keep diseases or harmful parasites from sweeping through the herds or flocks and wiping them out.

"I began as the first kind of veterinarian," Dr. Beamer said. "I treated small mammals and birds. Since I joined the staff at the Jackson Laboratory, my work is more like the second kind. I seldom treat individual animals, except in a research colony where an especially valuable breeding animal is sick. In that case, I try to find a cure for it and may treat it with antibiotics that are fed to it in water."

But, for the most part, Dr. Beamer is concerned with the health of entire colonies at a time. If a serious contagious disease should ever erupt among the thousands of mice in a breeding room, there would be no time to treat individual animals. In a part of her work, then, she does not treat the animals directly. She concerns herself with their environment. She constantly checks on the cleanliness of the materials with which the mice come in contact.

"Everything that goes into the mouse rooms is disinfected, but even then we don't feel secure," Dr. Beamer explained. "We always monitor the bottles and other equipment for harmful bacteria. Sometimes we discover that the washing machines are not working properly, and then the equipment is not as clean as it should be. We make sure that the problem is corrected at once."

Dr. Beamer and her staff depend heavily on the alertness of animal caretakers. The caretakers, as we have seen, make note of any unusual condition or behavior in their mice. If it is a possible mutant, the mouse is sent to the Mutant Mart. If it is obviously sick or injured, it is shipped to Dr. Beamer in the animal health laboratory. There she kills it humanely with gas and examines it to see if it had a contagious disease or a harmful parasite. If so, the room from which it came is carefully watched for any other signs of the problem.

"Despite all our watchfulness, a mouse sometimes shows up with pinworms or other parasites," Dr. Beamer said. "Pinworm eggs are very long-lived and sometimes they survive unnoticed in the fur of an animal family. Old mice don't groom themselves effectively, and these parasites may infest their fur."

Such infestations are very difficult, if not impossible, to stamp out once they have invaded a large colony of mice. Now, at the Jackson Laboratory, the staff is creating whole new colonies that are free of harmful organisms from the very beginning. One such collection of mice exists in the Animal Health Laboratory. It is called a hysterectomy-derived colony.

Work on this colony was begun in the 1960s. Scientists at the Animal Health Laboratory took newborn mice from their mothers. They were kept in germ-free compartments called isolators and hand-fed through medicine droppers. When the mice were weaned, they were free of contamination and were able to eat solid, sterilized food.

In an even more advanced program, the descendants of those hand-raised mice serve as foster mothers. They receive pups that have been taken from their natural mothers by an operation called a hysterectomy. The natural mothers are not as "clean" as the descendants of the hand-raised mice and so they might contaminate the pups while they are being born.

The staff in the Animal Health Laboratory observes the natural mothers during their pregnancy. The operation is performed on the day the pups would normally be born. A staff member removes the uterus from the natural mother, opens it, and lifts out the tiny pups. She gently rubs and rolls the pups until they turn pink and begin to breathe.

Meanwhile, a "clean" foster mother has been prepared to receive them. This female has been mated so that she will have pups of her own just before the "hysterectomy-derived" pups are brought to her cage. Her own pups are removed while she is out of the cage, and the other pups put in their place. She will then raise the new pups as if they were her own. These hysterectomy-derived mice are eagerly bought by other institutions because they are known to be free from disease and harmful organisms.

Dr. Beamer and her colleagues take every precaution to see that they are kept that way. The barriers between this colony of mice and the outside world are the strictest at the Jackson Laboratory. Scientists who enter this lab must first take a shower and put on sterilized clothing, caps, gloves, and face masks.

Hysterectomy-derived mice are in demand all over the world. Researchers who are performing especially delicate experiments want mice that are free of

Every precaution is taken to fill the laboratory's need for uncontaminated research animals.

bacteria, viruses, and other organisms that might affect the outcome of their studies.

These mice also serve as guardians of the other colonies. Sometimes, for some special purpose, a new strain of mice is imported to the Jackson Laboratory from another institution. There is always the chance that the new mice will bring in a harmful disease with them.

"We put the imported animals into a plastic isolator for six weeks," Dr. Beamer said. "Then we humanely kill a few of the imported mice and take tiny pieces of living tissue from them. We inoculate this tissue into our clean mice. If, after a period of several days, anything happens to our mice, then we know that the new mice cannot be admitted."

It would seem that nothing more can be done to protect Jax Mice. But recently the staff has taken a further step that would not have been dreamed of only a few years ago.

10 · The Embryo Bank

Dr. Larry Mobraaten, a tall, dark-bearded man, is a research scientist at the Jackson Laboratory. He led his visitors down a narrow corridor and into a small laboratory across from his office. There he wheeled a refrigerator, about three feet in height, into the center of the lab.

It was not an ordinary refrigerator. Made of stainless steel, it was shaped like a thermos bottle, with an inner stainless-steel wall to create a vacuum. An alarm was attached to its lid, ready to ring if anything went wrong inside. Pasted to the front of the refrigerator were the names and home telephone numbers of scientists who were to be called in case of an emergency.

Dr. Mobraaten lifted the lid. A dense white cloud rose from the refrigerator as the outside air came into contact with the frozen contents inside. For a few moments it was impossible to see anything through the frosty vapor. It finally cleared, and the scientist was able to look down on the small, pie-shaped boxes tightly packed in circles inside the refrigerator.

"There are 100,000 mice in there," Dr. Mobraaten said. "To be more exact, there are 100,000 frozen embryos of mice in there. When they are thawed out—a year from now or even many years from now—many of the embryos will grow into mice. And those mice will then be able to produce young mice of their own."

The scientists at Jackson Laboratory have used their imaginations to solve many of the problems that occur during the raising of three million mice a year. None of these solutions is more exciting than the program that is directed by Dr. Mobraaten. By freezing embryos only three days after they have been conceived by their mothers, Mobraaten relieves the rest of the staff of having to care for thousands of mice that are not needed for research at the moment. He also relieves the staff of the fear that valuable strains of mice might be wiped out by fire or disease.

"We have some strains of mice at the Jackson Laboratory that aren't in much demand by scientists just now," Mobraaten explained. "They have been thoroughly studied in the past. But who knows? Ten years from now scientists may want to study them again for other reasons.

"In the meantime, just keeping hundreds of mice in each of these strains would require a great deal of space and a great deal of work. But, in just these two small refrigerators, we are keeping more than 200,000 embryos from over a hundred different stocks of mice. They are safe here from the disasters that might destroy living mice. But when we want them again, we

Dr. Larry Mobraaten is in charge of an exciting new program to preserve the lab's future supply of research mice.

only have to thaw them. Then many of them will grow into normal mice."

The whole process sounds simple enough as Dr. Mobraaten described it, but behind this modern miracle lies much imagination and attention to detail. Dr. Mobraaten is quick to admit that much of the credit for his program's success must go to the hard work and sound advice of other scientists. As part of his duties at the Jackson Laboratory, he travels widely to scientific conferences and keeps up with the work of scientists all over the world.

Mobraaten learned that in 1972 a British scientist and two Americans had developed a method of freezing and thawing the embryos of mice. This development had obvious advantages for the Jackson Laboratory, which was running short of space. The laboratory's director put Dr. Mobraaten in charge of finding the best ways to freeze embryos to solve the laboratory's problems. This is how it works:

The main challenge that Dr. Mobraaten and his colleagues face is to collect large numbers of embryos at one time. The process of freezing and thawing is difficult. Some embryos will not survive. With many embryos to work with, the scientists will be more likely to achieve success.

The parent mice are carefully selected. Between twenty and fifty young females of each inbred strain at the lab are chosen just after they have been weaned. They are mated with their brothers or other closely related males.

The scientists then inject each of the females with

sex hormones. *Hormones*, which are chemical substances produced by the body's cells, control the behavior of other cells. In this case, the hormones cause the female mice to produce an exceptionally large number of eggs.

Three days after the mice are mated, the scientists collect the embryos. At this time each embryo consists of only eight identical cells. The whole embryo is about one-tenth of a millimeter in diameter and can only be seen with a microscope.

The female mice are killed before the operation. Because their uterus and oviduct are removed while collecting the embryos, they would be of no further use as experimental animals.

"Killing experimental animals is a touchy subject, but perhaps less so with mice than with cats and dogs," Dr. Mobraaten said. "I believe it should be dealt with in an honest manner. I, personally, do not like having to kill animals. But as a scientist I realize it is necessary, or one would not be able to carry out important experiments. At the Jackson Laboratory we try to do this in the most humane way that is practical."

Using a syringe, the scientists flush the embryos from the oviduct into a small container called a "watchglass." Then the scientists draw out the embryos from the watchglass with a *pipette*, which is a narrow glass tube that works by suction and lifts tiny living things from one container to another. In this way, fifty embryos are transferred to a small plastic vial that contains a saline solution.

Each vial holds between ten and fifty embryos. They are placed in a series of ice baths that gradually lowers their temperature. The shock of too sudden a change in temperature would be likely to kill the embryos. When they are thoroughly chilled, just to the point where ice forms, the plastic vials are capped and put into a small freezing chamber, where their temperature is again lowered gradually to $-8°$ C $(18°F)$. At this point, the scientists remove the vials from the freezing chamber and place them in pie-shaped, cardboard packages that fit neatly into the round racks in the refrigerators.

"The embryos are kept frozen in there by liquid nitrogen," Dr. Mobraaten explained. "The liquid nitrogen evaporates very quickly. If the supply should run low when no one is around, that alarm on the lid will go off. Whoever hears the alarm can reach one of us scientists at home by calling the numbers that are fastened to the outside of the refrigerators. Someone will arrive in time to add more liquid nitrogen and keep the embryos from thawing out. We take no chances with these valuable strains of mice."

After a strain has been frozen for several weeks, the scientists thaw those in one vial to make certain that all is well. This process must also be gradual.

"Very few of the embryos are killed when we freeze them," Dr. Mobraaten said. "But the process of thawing them and getting them to resume their growth is a very delicate operation. Embryos are so fragile at this stage that many of them do not survive.

In all, about one-fourth of the embryos are lost in one way or another. But we are trying to improve our methods and cut down on the losses."

The vial containing the embryos is removed from the refrigerator. It is placed in the freezing chamber, where the temperature is gradually raised. When the vial has thawed, the scientists use a pipette to draw out the embryos and put them into small tubes. The scientists add a nourishing liquid that is made from a special recipe developed at Jackson Laboratory. This substance is similar to the nourishment that embryos receive in their mother's uterus.

The scientists carefully watch the embryos. If the embryos begin to grow normally, they are ready to be restored to their natural environment, which is the uterus of a mature female mouse.

The scientists select healthy young females from the same mouse strain that produced the embryos. These females are allowed to mate with sterile males. This mating brings the females into a condition that very closely resembles pregnancy—except that they are not truly pregnant.

The females are given an injection of an anesthetic, which causes them to lose consciousness.

Then the scientists perform delicate surgery on the unconscious females. A small cut is made in an animal's back. The uterus is gently drawn to the opening and held in place by sterile thread. Using a tiny pipette, the scientist who is performing the operation injects the embryos into the uterus through a small hole made by a hypodermic needle. The uterus is then put back into place in the mouse's body and the skin is sealed with clamps.

At this point, the embryos resume their normal growth. It is almost as if nothing has changed in their brief existence. Weeks, perhaps years, may have passed since they were conceived, and their real mothers are no longer alive. Yet now they take up where they left off and keep developing until their new mother gives birth to them in a normal way.

Yet even then Dr. Mobraaten and his colleagues are not satisfied that the process has been a success.

"It will still be some time before we are certain that the stocks of any one particular strain are preserved for the future," Dr. Mobraaten said. "When these embryos grow into healthy young mice and are weaned from their foster parents, we mate them with other mice that once were frozen embryos, too. If these mice are able to produce healthy young of their own,

"Loop-tail" is one of the rare strains of mice that may be preserved in the embryo "bank."

then we know that the other embryos still in the refrigerator can be brought back to life to do the same thing."

The scientists at Jackson Laboratory hope some day to build a "bank" of every mutant strain of mice in the world. Mutant mice, wherever they are found—perhaps in China, Australia, or the Soviet Union—will be brought to Dr. Larry Mobraaten's laboratory if the plan is successful. There the embryos will be frozen and kept safe from all possible disasters. If, at any time in the future, scientists need a mouse of any mutant strain they will be able to withdraw it from the embryo bank at the Jackson Laboratory.

11 · Traveling Mice

At the beginning of every week a large, air-conditioned truck pulls up to the shipping room at the Jackson Laboratory. Cartons of valuable cargo are wheeled out to the truck and carefully loaded inside. The doors are closed and the truck drives back to the mainland and down the coast toward Boston, New York, and Washington.

A shipment of Jax Mice is on its way to waiting scientists in many parts of the world.

Like other activities at the laboratory, the shipping of Jax Mice begins with the animal caretakers in the breeding rooms. For several days the caretakers have been watching the litters of young mice in their cages. Some strains of mice mature very quickly and are ready to leave their parents by the time they are three weeks old. Most strains are weaned by the age of four weeks.

In the mornings, as the caretakers go about changing the colonies into fresh cages, they check the cards on each cage. If they see that a litter of young mice has reached the weaning age, they remove them

A weaning cage.

from their parents. They lift each young animal in turn with their forceps, note whether it is a male or a female, and then put it into a large weaning cage with other members of its sex.

A weaning cage usually holds twenty young mice. The males of some strains of mice, however, are fierce fighters. If they feel crowded, they will fight each other, and some of the mice will be injured or killed. Smaller numbers of males in these strains are held in the weaning cages.

Meanwhile, workers elsewhere at the Jackson Laboratory are preparing for the shipment of the weaned mice. Orders for Jax Mice arrive regularly from almost every state in the Union, as well as from many foreign countries. These orders come from scientists at research and educational institutions. The scientists order the mice by the names and numbers of the various strains. One scientist may want a hundred normal mice shipped every week for six months. Another scientist may order only mutants, such as dystrophic or dwarf mice.

Clerks in the order department record the orders on computers. The Jackson Laboratory's freight agency is also notified so that it can make the proper shipping arrangements at airports. Shipping labels are prepared for every order.

Other workers put together the shipping cartons. These cartons are especially designed for the shipment of Jax Mice. They consist of sterilized sheets of corrugated paper board that are folded and stapled to form a box. A fine filter is stapled over breathing holes in the cartons to strain out harmful organisms in the air.

Workers at the lab prepare the shipping cartons that will carry Jax Mice all over the world.

The entire carton is lined with tough wire screen to prevent the mice from chewing through the carton.

By this time, the caretakers have sent the weaning cages filled with mice to the shipping area. Other trained workers prepare the cartons for the mice. They line the bottoms with wood shavings. Then they open cans of food, a specially prepared shipping diet, and drop it into the cartons. The food consists of a mixture of grain and water developed by the laboratory's scientists and packaged at a nearby sardine cannery.

"It tastes pretty good," said a man who supervises its preparation. "It's a little like Indian pudding. Anyway, the mice seem to like it."

Each mouse is examined once more before going into a carton. The shipping clerk checks to see that all the mice are of the same size and appearance. He or she then makes sure that each animal is of the sex that has been ordered, and does not seem to be sick or injured. As many as fifty young mice travel in one carton, though there may be as few as five if they are fighting males. A worker staples the carton shut and the mice are on their way to the truck.

The first stop is a freight distribution terminal near Boston. There the cartons are redirected. Some go to Logan International Airport where they are put aboard planes that will take them to distant parts of the United States or to institutions in South America, Europe, or Asia. Others are distributed by truck to institutions in the Boston area and other cities along the East Coast.

The prices of Jax Mice vary, depending on the

difficulty in producing them. A mouse from a normal inbred strain may sell for two dollars. A mutant, such as a dystrophic mouse, may sell for thirty-eight dollars or more.

Jax Mice, raised in comfort, may discover the hardships of life once they have been shipped from the laboratory. Mice that are caught in a heat wave on the way to a new home may not survive. During one recent winter, a large shipment of Jax Mice was snowbound at an airport when planes could not take off for several days. The mice, running out of food and in a badly weakened condition, had to be humanely destroyed.

The mice do not always receive careful handling in shipment, either. There are warnings on the cartons to carry them gently and not turn them upside down. But sometimes the people who move cargoes treat the mice as if they were bundles of old newspapers.

"I happened to be at the airport one day when they were loading Jax Mice aboard a plane," one of the laboratory's scientists said. "I saw a worker carrying cartons in each hand, and they were hanging down so that all of the mice and their food must have been tumbled together at one end of the carton."

Scientists at the Jackson Laboratory want to know what happens to the mice once they leave their care. They have experimented with various devices that make a record of what happens to the cartons. One of these instruments is called an impact recorder. It is sealed into the carton with the mice. It consists of a small metal box that contains a needle, a timing device, and some very sensitive tape.

If the box is dropped, tilted, or turned upside down, the needle moves on the tape and leaves marks on it. When this instrument reaches its destination, scientists can tell not only how often the carton was handled roughly, but even the time at which it was shaken up. They can show this evidence to the shippers, who are expected to find ways to prevent careless handling of the cartons in the future.

Traveling mice, the laboratory's staff believes, ought to get the best of care, too.

12 · Mice for the Future

The story that appeared on the front pages of leading newspapers not long ago told of an exciting development. Scientists at Yale University had planted genes from a virus into the embryos of mice. When the mice were born, the scientists found that these "foreign genes" had become part of the animals' bodies.

The research at Yale was still in its early stages, but scientists believe that it will become important in the fight against disease. How can the joining of a virus with a mouse contribute to human health? The point is that it now becomes possible to plant damaged human genes in mice, too. Scientists can grow a colony of mice with these defective genes and then study human diseases in great detail.

The mice used in the experiment at Yale came from the Jackson Laboratory. For many years, much of the research on genetics and human disease that took place in the United States used fruit flies and other tiny organisms. Clarence Cook Little, as we have seen, was one of the first scientists to see the usefulness of inbred strains of mice.

Since its foundation, the Jackson Laboratory has become a major center of mouse research and mouse production. It may become the world's "mouse bank" as well, as its scientists freeze embryos for future use.

Many more mice will be needed in the coming years for research such as the important work at Yale. This means that the methods of raising useful mice must keep pace with the methods of medical research. Scientists at the Jackson Laboratory are finding new ways to produce mice more efficiently.

Two of the most important problems to solve in raising millions of mice are space and cleanliness. We have already seen some of the ways in which these problems are being solved. Much space is saved by freezing embryos and storing them in small refrigerators. Food, clothing, cages, floors, and walls are disinfected to prevent the mice from being contaminated. Dr. Edwin Les has found new ways to deal with these problems.

"Until now, we have been successful in disinfecting objects like food or clothing or cages," Dr. Les said. "It hasn't been as simple to provide clean air to the animal in its cage."

The staff at the Jackson Laboratory has always struggled to keep polluted air from entering the breeding rooms. Purified air is pumped into the rooms through large overhead pipes called ducts. In some rooms, smaller ducts carry the air directly into the cages so that the mice have a constant supply of fresh air. The air pressure in the rooms is kept at a higher level than the air outside. In that way, air flows out of

Thousands of mice create their own air pollution. Dr. Edwin Les has invented a new system for changing the air in cages.

the rooms when a door is opened, while the unpurified air outside cannot get in.

One problem remained. Thousands of mice living together in a room create air pollution of their own. There is a strong odor from a colony of mice, arising mainly from the ammonia produced by bacteria that grow in their feces and urine. In addition, a great deal of almost invisible dust drifts from the cages. The dust comes from tiny particles of feed, bedding, and *dander*, which is tiny flakes of hair and skin cast off by the bodies of mice.

"Infections can be passed around through the mouse colony by this kind of dust," Dr. Les said. "It's also troublesome for human beings. Some of the scientists and caretakers are allergic to the dust. We encourage these people to wear charcoal-filled face masks while they are working around mice."

No manufacturer made the kind of equipment that would individually isolate mouse cages in the breeding rooms. But scientists, by nature, are problem-solvers. After a number of experiments, Dr. Les developed a new kind of rack for holding the cages. The large duct that brings fresh air to the rooms is attached directly to tubes in the hollow shelves. Holes in the shelves allow fresh air to pass into each cage. Stale air flows out through other holes into a second series of ducts that carry away the dust and odors.

In the years ahead, all of us will read about exciting new discoveries in medical research. Scientists will add to our understanding of genes and heredity. They will find ways to help people who suffer from cancer. They will be able to explain why some people are likely to inherit physical defects—and perhaps even mental and emotional defects—from their parents.

October 10, 1980, was a day that will never be forgotten at the Jackson Laboratory. On that morning, the news was flashed around the world from Stockholm, Sweden, that Dr. George Snell was one of three scientists who were to receive the Nobel Prize for Medicine. Dr. Snell had come to the laboratory in 1935. Through a series of breeding experiments there, he discovered that certain strains of inbred mice were able to accept the transplant of living tissue from other mice. But some mice rejected these transplants.

Dr. Snell continued his experiments for many years. He looked for the genes that caused some mice

A half century ago few people understood the work of specialists such as Dr. George Snell and his co-workers at the Jackson Laboratory. But in 1980 Dr. Snell was among the winners of the prestigious Nobel Prize for Medicine.

to accept tissue transplants, and other mice to reject them. His work helped to make possible the transplant of kidneys and other organs between unrelated human beings. His reward was the highest honor that a scientist can receive—the Nobel Prize.

Other men and women have shared in the satisfaction of taking part in revolutionary medical research at the laboratory. The people who care for the animals and discover the mutants, as well as those who provide the right conditions for raising these valuable animals, are an important part of the story, too. A young animal caretaker summed up the feelings of her fellow workers.

"I like hearing people talk about the Jackson Laboratory," she said. "It makes me feel good to know that I am a part of what is going on there."

Index